Gathering Firewood

THE WESLEYAN POETRY PROGRAM: VOLUME 75

Gathering Firewood

NEW POEMS AND SELECTED

BY David Ray

Wesleyan University Press

MIDDLETOWN, CONNECTICUT

Acknowledgement is gratefully made to Cornell University Press, the publisher of *X-Rays: A Book of Poems* (1965) and of *Dragging the Main and Other Poems* (1968), from which collections selected poems are here reprinted, and to Barre Publishers, Columbia University Press, Grossman Publishers, Latitudes Press and Random House, the publishers of anthologies in which certain other poems in this book were first published; and to the following periodicals, in the pages of which a number of other poems in this book were first published: *Accent, Ambit, The Antioch Review, The Atlantic Monthly, Black Swamp, Centennial Review, Chicago Review, Choice, Crazy Horse, December, Epoch, Field, The Florida Poetry Review, Foxfire, The Greenfield Review, The Iowa Review, The Journal of Popular Culture, Kamadhenu, The Kansas City Star, Kumquat, The Nation, New American Review, Northwest Minnesota Review, Northwest Review, Poetry, The Quarterly Review of Literature, The Seneca Review, Transpacific* and *Twentieth Century.*

The publisher gratefully acknowledges the support of the publication of this book by the Andrew W. Mellon Foundation.

Library of Congress Cataloging in Publication Data

Ray, David, 1932—
    Gathering firewood.

    (The Wesleyan poetry program, v. 75)
    I. Title.
PS3568.A9G3   811'.5'4   74–5968
ISBN 0–8195–2075–6
ISBN 0–8195–1075–0 (pbk.)

Manufactured in the United States of America

First edition

For

Suzanne Judy
Samuel Cyrus David
Sapphina James
Wesley Jean
Winifred Catherine

& for

Cyrus Colter, Marie Eastman, Francisco Gomez
and Alvin Suslick

Contents

Gathering Firewood

Gathering Firewood

At the over-matured *sushi*
The master
Is full of regret.
                              — Buson

Soft you, a word or two before you go;
I have done the State some service and they know't:
No more of that: I pray you in your letters,
When you shall these unlucky deeds relate,
Speak of me as I am; nothing extenuate,
Nor set down aught in malice: then you must speak.
                              — *Othello*

Not faded, if images are all we have.
They can be no more faded than ourselves.
                              — Wallace Stevens

For the Suicides

It's like an orchid.
It suffers on.
It is like ice
on pines.
You say you dance
among glass mobiles,
knowing it all has to break
soon,
the sheer satin
of your face, soon,
soon, you know.
A lifetime knots
into your chest
or hurting set
of bones.
What's to say?
I've been among the haves
and have-nots.
The haves have less.
I get lonely as hell
not being able to tell
you girls
everything I see
on your hurt faces,
letting you go without me
where the world
will hurt you more. You're
Orchids on the roofs of cars
to pin on a black lapel,
Daddy's coat.

Chekhov

If I feel that you've
      invaded our privacy,
made our faces sting like nettles,
If I can't find my friends
      or find my life in the dark,
If you've reduced me to tears,
If I know not now
      where to go
      —toward the destructive
      —toward the fragmentary
If you've spoken
      through desperate hands
those vases that break
      those marriages
      those friendships cold
        bitter and lonely,
those partings in the forest,
If I have lost her again and again
I see now,
      Chekhov,
        it is all your fault.

A cellar would keep jars cool.
You promised to dig one.
You could dig one with a mule
And a piece of iron.
But first you had to break the mule
And that was a mean business.
But you kept your vow
And later the mule
Ran away, flipping the iron
End over end
Scaring me like everything
Else you and the mule did.

And she bore jars into the damp earth
Like a Cretan girl.
She placed the jars
Upon shelves that are fallen
Here, all broken in this
Agamemnon's tomb.
And I have come to dig the shards
Out of the wet leaves
And find what you left.
Here are the rusty cans
Our mother fed us from
When she denied the breast,
Small dugs that I remember,
With nipples like figs.
Here are the rusty springs
Of our bed, both brother
And sister.
And here is a rusty ring

Like a half-moon,
The basin she washed us in.

You were indeed the most cursed
Of parents.
The deep rains hurt at your house
And at last washed it down
The hill.
The open fire in the middle
Of your dirt floor
Burned at your poor bed
Like a rich man's eyes.
In the day you went out and broke
Stones.
The mule learned to turn away
From the ruins
And salt stains on the earth.
And stunned by your own failure
When you left, Christ's life
Ago, you left the gates
Wide open. Iron. Gates.

Archeology

I find the old farm,
dig in the ruins, barn,
wagon, smokehouse, caved in
well,
find the rusty three-pronged
pitchfork,
first relic found
that linked Grampa
to the sea.

A Ruined Shack in the Hills

A man and a woman were up here
in the hills.
They broke rocks.
They broke each other.
They made of the scrub oak
a labyrinth
for finding the bleached bone
of a cow, a pelvis.
And yellow daisies grow,
as over a battlefield.

Nowata

The town needed me.
It drove me on. Winters,
I slid on the iced rails
Of streetcars.
Summers, I dished stew
Down at the Oasis Grill
and Poolhall, another place
The decent folk
Wouldn't want to look
For love or stew or snooker.
Ah, little did rich old Landers
Know how good that stew was,
Called "Mulligan."
The town needed me,
Desperately.
One June I mowed the whole
Cemetery, then swept the stones.
It's a wonder I didn't build that town.
But I return, and there's still
No town built there
Nor anyone sowing the seeds
Of *Communitas*
On the right side of the tracks.
But I cross over and stare
Where chickens peck
At the ruins of black Myrtle's shack.

It is only nickels and dimes we ring up.
And pennies.
We won't take paper.
Our fortunes must be built entirely
Of pennies and nickels and dimes.
Not a single quarter on the heap!
Not a fifty-cent piece, with the eagle
Of the Republic!
Of human hairnets we have spoken.
Of Mickey Rooney, tinted,
Smiling in tweed
The year he met Ava Gardner
We are discoursing.
Betty Grable we are still propping
On the knickknack,
Looking back at us
Over her shoulder, standing
In her white bathing suit.
Here shoelaces of any length
Are available for the last time!
We are going out of business
Entering the graves
Where ceramic saltshakers will surround us.
We will lie forever on pillows
Embroidered with the names
Of seaside resorts
And verses loud enough to wake us
When we want.

gives up dignity,
cries aloud in public,
gets down on the floor
with the children of light
and of darkness,
weeps openly
or in secret,
yearns for a face
that is gone or
a face in the mirror,
defends the assassin,
sees only glory,
sees no end
to the suffering,
no opening up,
no gifts coming,
finds meaning in wheat,
mostly isn't wanted,
is victim to anything,
a cow, a wooden bucket,
can stand in the doorway
and gawk,
weeps at bikes leaning
together, scrawls notes
madly, shoves them
into books,
is lunatic, wonders
which will come first,
the collapse of
capitalism or the emancipation
of man,
can be a gatekeeper,

can paint plates,
can hear the terrible meanings
go on speaking,
can stand offering spirit
saying would do anything for

and what do *we* do
how do we pay back
the touched life
that spirit pure as
the baby rabbit

by edict saying
it shall not happen
this miracle of
human closeness

Catfish

Foxtails of grass
make a wall
we can hardly see through
to the rosy West.
Those who stand on the road
with me
are dusty from our civilization.
We are all going down
to the river to see fish
we can't eat
and to hear singing the last
songs of the farm,
to see if the books
have come floating yet,
from the fine towns.

Father and Son and Bedsprings

For this you hauled them up the hill,
the bedsprings,
first on the truck, then on your back.
You put them on the dirt floor
sharecroppers have.
And round the house you made the clearing.
You clear away scrub oak, white spiders.
You clear away the other women,
they're back in town.
You clear away even the memory of cousins,
horses, pigs, your own cock in your hand.
You clear away disease: even Death would go away
so you can grunt in the night like a mystic.
Now, sinking into her,
it is like clearing a gigantic space
in the universe and going away into it.
But not you return: for this is the wire
that cuts your life in two:
now there is the hateful child, the squall
and never the woman's smile.
She buttons her dress and never smiles.
You try to remember what it was.
It was good. It was like eating the fields.
Now the child has that.
And the child lets the oak grow back
and the white spiders crawl.
Now you yourself have to crawl,
oak leaves with dust touching your face.
You think of it: the child will come back,
after the bedsprings have rusted
ten million years. He will jump up and down
on them.

He will joke with some beautiful woman.
He will think "My father can't have her."
He will have that over the father.
He will say "Look here, here are the bedsprings
I was conceived on. Would you believe it?"
He will kick them.
He will discuss keeping them for a souvenir,
mounting them on plywood as a found object.
Though if he looked more closely he might find
the small bitter berry of his father.

The Family

Rounding up the family one chick
and kitten at a time, I see that even
the fly on the barn wall becomes
someone for whom I was searching

At the Spring

And the sun on her back,
The water so cold. I have forgotten
To love her as I should.
Is there anything quite like the edge of a breast
— like a little moon —
Swinging out at a woman's side
As she bends to the water

Season's Greetings

Sister! And others to whom
I owe this least
obeisance of saying what
movies I've seen
or what I ate for the day
or how the weather darkens,
avoiding politics
and love and the
itchy ass: sisters and
dearest slightest acquaintances
(and mother, and father
who still so strangely live),
please forgive
me — in building
this tiny nest which I make,
this ludicrous, wobbling
nest that barely
keeps me alive,
I have had to steal
all the words
I could get, words
that would never make
sheep, to be herded
into those letters you need.

Wesley's Apple

Holding the pencil in her fist
to draw an apple
she shows me a hand that is
itself an apple, a small pale apple.

Analysis

Here is my great book.
It is called Paradise Lost
(I regain it as I talk)
Naked as jaybirds,
Adam and Eve are all alone,
except for me.
I crawl and see them
from the floor.
At noon my Mom
is always eating.
It might as well
be what I say,
or me.
She talks to Dad
right after. I'm
despised
and might as well
be killed
with a hard hoe
(work came before
sin) The hate
of Satan
is what I know.
My hands are small and wet
with tears.
The telling of this tale
has taken years.

A Midnight Diner by Edward Hopper

Your own greyhounds bark at your side.
It is you, dressed like a Sienese,
Galloping, ripping the gown as the fabled
White-skinned woman runs, seeking freedom.
Tiny points of birches rise from hills,
Spin like serrulate corkscrews toward the sky.
In other rooms it is your happiness
Flower petals fall for, your brocade
You rediscover, feel bloom upon your shoulder.

And freedom's what the gallery's for.
You roam in large rooms and choose your beauty.
Yet, Madman, it's your own life you turn back to:
In one postcard purchase you wipe out
Centuries of light and smiles, golden skin
And openness, forest babes and calves;
You forsake the sparkler breast
That makes the galaxies; you betray
The women who dance upon the water

All for some bizarre hometown necessity!
Some ache still found within you!
Now it will go with you, this scene
By Edward Hopper and nothing else.
It will become your own tableau of sadness
Composed of blue and grey already there.
Over or not, this suffering will not say Hosanna.
Now a music will not come out of it.
Grey hat, blue suit, you are in a midnight
Diner painted by Edward Hopper.

Here is a man trapped at midnight underneath the El.

He's sought the smoothest counter in the world
And found it here in the almost empty street,
Away from everything he has ever said.
Now he has the silence they've insisted on.
Not a squirrel, not an autumn birch,
Not a hound at his side, moves to help him now.
His grief is what he'll try to hold in check.
His thumb has found and held his coffee cup.

Automat

One at one table,
one at another.

Her stray hair is stroked
(by her). He reads Wall St.

It's quite classic —
separate tables

brass glistens on,
polished spittoons

and reflected lights
a highway out to hell,

black as hell.
Extent of human reach, nihil,

and loneliness burning loud
like lamps left on

Speaking

Have I made the mistake
of trying to be too
                    transparent
to some human being?
Is this why we turn to
ducks that sail upon
the river and manage to
leave a pure V?
Everywhere behind us, grieving
waters . . .

My Poems

are like cedar shakes
which I let slip
from my fingers
one by one
in the middle of the ocean

Stopping near Highway 80

We are not going to steal the water-tower
in Malcom, Iowa,
just stop for a picnic right under it.
Nor need they have removed the lightbulb
in the city park
nor locked the toilet doors.
We are at peace, just eating and drinking
our *poco vino* in Malcom, Iowa,
which evidently once had a band
to go with its bandstand.
We walk down the street, wondering how
it must be to live behind the shades
in Malcom, Iowa, to peer out,
to remember the town as it was before
the expressway discovered
it, subtracted what would flow
on its river eastwards and westwards.
We are at peace, but when we go into the bar
in Malcom, Iowa, we find that the aunts
and uncles drinking beer have become
monsters and want to hurt us and we do
not know how they could have ever
taken out the giant breasts
of childhood or cooked the fine biscuits
or lifted us up high on the table
or have told us anything at all
we'd ever want to know
for living lives as gentle as we can.

In the Air-Force Museum

You were perplexed — walking through the B-29 —
that the yellow bomb said
BREATHING OXYGEN
How could the breath of life be in
a bomb? you asked, your hand
touching it, so worried
that life might be confused with death.
I said Don't worry, it's all right,
They only want to breathe
more so they can go on
and kill more — all is consistent
Alles in Ordnung

A Piece of Shrapnel

The Rock That Doesn't Break, she calls
it that, picks it up in a field of clover,
brushes off the mud, asks me what it is
but who am I to explain war to a five-
year-old, who myself see something which
even to touch is dangerous, it is so sharp
and unshiny. I can feel it wanting
to hurt, to whizz through the air, land
in a tangle, be sold and resold. I can feel
how restless it is, not having found after
all this search a grave, where it can rest
and not be picked up, once more estranged,
searching again through hands and delicate
faces. It is like a small, tired heart
begging not to be stolen still again from
this grave, which is in a field of clover.

The Indians near Red Lake

When the white man comes
he comes to see a grave,
to look at the little house
over the grave, to ask
how the dead can eat the food
placed there
and always we give him the same answer
"The same way, white man,
your dead can smell your flowers"

The white man is interested
only in death.
He cares nothing for the story
of the pregnant girls
digging the banana-shaped roots
of the yellow lily
with their toes, tucking one
in at the waist for good luck.

The white man wants to hear
about the German scalp
brought back in nineteen forty-five.
He wants to hear how
it was put on the Chief's grave
After three nights of scalpdance.
He is amused
to think the Chief may stroll
in the other world
with the Germans and the small Japanese
for servants.

He walks through the weeds of our yards
to see a grave.
He brings nothing
else, none of the friendship,
the fellowship we've spread our nets for
for years, in our yards,
beside the abandoned Buicks,
waiting for him to notice.

The nets go on catching spiders
and what the white man throws away as
he drives through, fast,
in his car.
We take our smiles to town,
but neither do they catch anything.
Out nets are dry.
Yet we watch them.

Driving through the Winnebago Reservation

The dusty road and store were Greek,
or my childhood's —
prices doubled for the poor, and fat pot
stoves to lug upon the back.
The white man's store was flyspray, kids
buying Kool-aid, the icebox full
of lunch meat, right next to Shell
No-Pest. Across the road a field of
broken down schoolbuses and a hearse
threw shattered mirrors toward the sky.
In the woods we almost cut
our toes on beer cans and wondered
why the shirt
was tied upon a tree, some
symbol of gaunt or giant suffering
or some checkered marking
for a crooked mind. We swam,
naked and alone, and a fish bit
my toe when we made love, all but
our shoulders under water.
From the looks of things ashore
he was the last fish living
there and not attracting flies
face up. But we were grateful
for the silence
that I broke like Krishna
when your large face left off watching
shores and skies.
We loved in poison waters and let
strange slime grow round us
as if we were already statues
in the forest. Later, unashamed

and smiling, we picked the yellow
water lilies that the Winnebago ate,
and cat-tails. We're old enough
at last to save our shame
for Presidents and politics,
and old enough to know that evil left
those houses on white concrete blocks —
with filigree of nets like spiders
in the sun that have caught just three old cars
and two Bemidji tourists looking,
with handbooks, for beads and a chief's grave.

For Judy

Laying the 'gilded loam' of your head
against my arm
I pray for us now and at the hour of our love

The Way We Were

Birds first,
we all bunched up on a branch,
two or three of us flying

off together, came back
to trees, made mistakes
thinking how to nest.

Dogprints on snow.
Flying round in dark
when we were crazy

we saw large view,
knew Goethe,
"whom a rose ensnared."

Spartanburg

These are pictures for the family album.
Here Billy's two and standing by the chickens.
Here we are standing in front of the
Watermelon wagon; the melons are like
Eggs, or bellies, or bombs. Here we are
Stooping in the field, planting
Our good deeds, sowing
So we can reap. Look at how little Billy
Follows his Daddy behind the plow!
Here Uncle Orville is cutting up a dog
Because he is bored and doesn't want
To go to the movie, or the whorehouse.
Here is Goldilocks, standing with her basket:
Orville wrote home about that, he shot her
Because she might have a grenade
In her basket.
And here stands the lady he saw in the street
Holding her baby who had a hole in its head.

In Hell

all journeys seem longer
images sharp, as you meant them to be
in heaven

The Potato-Eaters

We go walking along the railroad track,
stooping to pick up clinkers
to get close to those people
who were to others mere stones to count.
We lean over the bridge
to watch how the world takes them in its currents.
They float away, this the magic,
as their kisses and their potato-eating
were magic.
And at night no happiness
is quite complete without thought of them.
We want to embrace strangers
hoping it will somehow get through to *them* too,
the anonymous, the eaten by fire,
the swallowed by water, those burned
in fire and in water.
They disappeared, seeing America
in the distance. They saw all our light
as one would see a storm advancing,
insisting on silence concerning them.
They glow inside their stones.

Skid Row

Thin curtain bellowing out,
endlessly begging in the night.
And in the morning, the last pennies,
out of a can, for a plum.

W. C. W.

knew a poet
doesn't have to be on
his best behavior

all the time, has
many bad
poems, very
lifelike, very

relaxed, and breaks
into song
only on occasion

as all folks do,
walking along

Such a World to Fail

Arthritic fingers,
    the chasm of mind.
Williams as one-
    cornered Ma
of the Sung
    dynasty, who painted
only mind, void,
    the soft nothing,
though scholars
    and a dog
might stand bemused,
    cliffside.
In this valley
    we see regrets
everywhere,
    the nest made
of flung hair
    and the frail
hell of hands.
How our fingers shake,
    our weak eyes
failing the world.

The Archaic

If something is archaic
all edges have been dulled
broken by the sea
and yet
some trace
of the old life
must be left,
some evidence that this white stone
was once a lion's
leg, or the base
of an intricate temple.
If that life
surviving wind and sea
does not lead
us back, in some effort
to rediscover, retracking
our own steps,
then this something
we have found
in its desolation
is not truly
archaic.

To be archaic
is to exist
in a state of transition
between a silent life
and a whispering death:
even our own
bodies when we stop and
listen closely
seem to be giving off
some aura
of the genuinely
archaic.

In Greece

Approaching that fantastic
space behind all men and women
(still holding their stone robes)
you see that there is only one
relationship; two figures in the
foreground, one range of mountains
in the immense distance, with
nothing in between.
Are you sure you can face it?
Here we have our pain —
our candles, and a dark sea,
our faces growing white like statues.

With Samuel

We ignore the barbed wire
from an old war.
The donkeys bray all night.
My son is the first man
to see the holy moon,
the wrinkled sea
that will shipwreck
no saint tonight.
"It's the right moon," he says.
He is my friend.
I lift him high, so high.
A few flowers survive.

At Delos

I have come to protest
above the empty treasury shaft,
the deep quarry where they came,
and I stand before the archaic holy
lions with their round jaws
and take the sign out of my pocket,
unfold it, hold it up
and let them see it, let them
read my placard — it is written
on the back of an old valentine —
Now I am moving down the line
of old emperors,
bearded, whipped by rain,
their faces enduring in tobacco-
colored marble,
half fallen into the sea,
here where even the winds turned round.

Through Museum Glass

Bronze greaves of 5th century
B. C.
I still have knees for

Sculpture

People can remove themselves like paintings
Or join one another as sculpture.
We are part of the same statue together.
I can feel the basalt nature of our skin.
We have been chipped at together
Made to cling as one
Bound ourselves inward against the weather.
You were the first to look upon me
Without cynicism in your eyes
And then you joined me in this stone.
Now we can go back to childhood.
Now I know you would rather sink
Into the earth with me than be free.
Nothing can wrench you away now.
As we crouch here upon the earth
Our moments come home to us.
Don't be surprised that they are still
Cold from their loneliness.

After Sappho

Let us live so that the rust of our bodies
Will rub off on others, in future years.

The Shoelaces

Bending down to tie my son's shoelace
Where he sits in the stroller
In a bar in Spain, I see below me a jumble
Of geologic layers and rivers
Of time: there are the cross-
Bars, holding the miniature and mystical
Cities; there is my own tweed
Sleeve, steel-toed shoes going back
To freight-loading days, and there is
This little man standing up,
Drunk with enthusiasm for a sick world.

Discovering Old Hotels

We are not the first
to put time on this room
wash in their sink
put love into
this bed
and walk across
these creaking floors.
Such furniture
as this
the politicians
forgot to axe and
in the red light
of the fire exit
we hear voices drifting
over the transom
talking of wars
that are gone
so we can sleep
a little

If It Speaks It Speaks to Me

I was the victim of that saying and so
I went searching for certain street corners in Vienna
and felt like a tourist in my own home
where the edges should have been brushed
smooth years ago. When I walked through
castles the murder holes glowed above me
and the dungeons had waited
a thousand years to hold me.
The river was heavier than ever
and conversation hurt round like birds
calling forth filth and anger
from faces of the dead.
They would give us no peace
but kept offering us cups with bizarre designs
and forests

Breaking My Glasses on Clear Glass

I was trying to get to the sunlit place.
My eyes were focussed way out there
where Plato said the truth was
and walking, as over mountains,
I wanted to get to the circle
and the triangle and the infinite
parallel lines.
For years birds have been broken,
wing by wing.
My head is where it hurt me,
this thin reality.

Ada

We find her on a sidestreet
of Sapulpa, living
in a little tomb her son
built of stones.
We walk in, under
the catalpa tree, and
she cradles our faces
in her hands,
asking where we've been.
"I'll cook for You-uns," she says,
knowing we came for the old days,
knowing we can see reflected
in her eyes
the clock and the day-bed
and the fields through
the window, with cousins
stooping there.

In the front bedroom where
she slept with Grampa
the dog with the chipped ear
listens.
The stove blazes through isinglass.
We have found for a moment
this woman with her hair
in a bun, who stood with Grampa
before a giant wooden wheel
that never went anywhere,
while we hopped round like chickens.

Thoughts of Malcolm Lowry

At least I can still tie my own shoes.
"No, dear," said his wife, "put your sock
on first."
Mine still match five days
out of seven.
The Zenith heavenly circle
still blares out Scarlatti
as it did in Chicago
when we suffered,
bought tin pans
in dimestores.
If we heard of a new form
of suffering
— one with the resiny smell
of pines —
we had to have it, then.
Other hells were strung like jewels.
The men wrote, the girls loved.
The beds squeaked, the cats scratched.
Nausea came out in a new edition.
Malcolm Lowry fell asleep
floating on his back in the Bay of Naples,
some womb,
got frightful burns.
No book is worth it and
I wouldn't slit your belly for a book.

A beauty that embarrasses,

Tibor's wife, for instance,
whom he holds by the elbow
as she stands out in the busy traffic.
Her beauty is so intense and heavy
that Tibor, holding her arm, is
embarrassed — that battle should be over,
the apples and cabbages picked.
Men who surround such women are tired.
They have saddened and worn out
before their wives
who are of some hardy variety.
Such women looked down on us when we were boys.
We saw then that they were gross
flowers kept in opaque greenhouses,
tended with gloved hands.

She makes happiness on the last day
of the world.
Her heart is innocent like a little bird's.
And if she has lovers they are like
the wandering ghost of yourself.
"She makes beautiful salad dressing,"
Tibor says, making a remark
that is a kind
of continuity between your thoughts
and his.

In Heraklion

When we counted out the few coins in our purse
at the hotel desk
and found out we had enough to take a bath
they did not guess what riches we took with
us (hidden in your coat, hidden in
me) up the stairway
and what laughter we surrounded ourselves with
(all by ourselves)
when we sank down to the floor by the radiator
trying to get warm
turning to each other because the radiator
was cold, because only hair warmed me.
That day, or the day before, we had sat
upon the throne of Minos — first me
then you.
We rode the bus back from Knossos.
We bore the faint mark of the king
upon our passports. We walked through
the mobbed streets of that city
built for Hercules. We smelled
the hot foods, the lamb they were cutting
and no one guessed I was luckier
than that king who was not in love
so they didn't try to take you away
from me and it was easy
to pay for a room and watch my
princess sink into the ancient pool.

Movements

Country —
making a museum out of walking around,
porcelain dogs, rusty bridge
of old Korean bronze,
windmill that turns, Uffizi
ditches
and Prado tar —
with pieces torn out of my own life.

Town —
making a museum out of driving around,
hot-dog stand so hot it burned down,
McDonald fine orange wickets,
billionth burger of the economy,
and plenitude of wild dimestores.

For Søren Kierkegaard

(whose desk I saw in Copenhagen,
stabbed with rage, even in the time
of his greatness)

These men I meet
in my day (call it that) —
Would you illuminate,
transcend,
find best?
They'd start on you
hunchback
unholy coat and porkpie hat,
then cast you
"straightway down
into the lower domains
of pettiness," ignore
you like an Indian.

But we, you and me, we
could walk
along old railroad
tracks, no trains,
and I could show
Sherwood Anderson's grief,
grim warehouses,
defeated fields,
crucifixion poles
in dark wind,
and you could share out
of that bundle on your back
a few of those bones.

Spain

Age helps.
I no longer ask Do we have it good
Or Are we covering up our problems
I just get mellow and
My cock's in a sweet decline.
And at night the stars swing out
From Africa, delighted,
Over the Kiosko.

The New Widow

The new gloves, veil,
smile that is tempered in an hour.
Black hand pushing past fruit,
a woman runneth over
out of this darkness.

Back in America

The river flows on
with its hot hogfat.
A smudge lies on everything
on yin and yang meaning
where bellies join spiders,
grey beams of old life.
Turtles on concrete walk into
the middle lane, having little chance.
Bus station hamburgers, sad
gals living on tips,
dark eyes on
wrinkled women, everyone
striving to learn
something from messages on
dimestore crocks or brocade
pillows or each other's struck
faces, or on the backs of trucks
bearing pure bombs, toward
the West.

Ravenna

And what did we see, high up there
in mosaics
but the old cousins, Beatrice, Edris, Alice
holding cups of gold, their haloes
awkward like the strawhats
they wore in the beanfields

Floors

Dawn floats out from downtown
finding at last
the farmers' market where we sleep
on mats or where we lie
thinking, thinking.
I want to leave a note saying
World how deeply you have hurt me
and yet I know
I have done it all.
Who is to be the child?
I stare at fences that said nothing
when we were tortured.
I want to talk my way back
into the children's barracks
so I can look through the window
once more
crawling over barbed wire
crawling down skyscrapers, finding
the one who kept me
weeping. I will use again
the slant road, the giant chair,
the cold red bricks our world
was made of —
all poor, pure objects.

An Unknown Wilderness

"This keeps night here,
and throws an unknown wilderness about me."
— Beaumont and Fletcher

I

Time we are not together
    is not time, it is the soup
        of wildwood, it is the memory
of pogroms, it is eyes to the ground
    looking for bread in the dust
        it is looking to the skies
for terror, finding the past there
    it is not being mothered, finding
        no hand in the night

II

Simply a man and a woman going
over the hill together
And I always know whether this bus
is going away from you
or briefly round the curve of sea
toward you. This bus and I will not
become an animal nosing,
burrowing toward you
through mountains, over the sea
So I am an old man shivering
sitting in a bus seat weeping
because I see a man and a woman
going over the hill together
into their poverty, their blessings

III

The pale morning light has a way
of breaking itself up into stars
Through the planks of the roof
it did this, all alone
though I was without you and couldn't
make anything happen. They left me there
the skies and the cliffs of the world
left me standing bemused
talking to myself, wondering where they had gone
and ahead of me there was an edge
a half-blossoming

IV

Tables I looked at because they could have been our
Tables. O thou freshly gathered
Then fallen
In the dark, in a strange city
I go on talking to you
out loud, out loud

V

Once you were like an archaic statue
And I found past time upon you
I was the child playing at the base, the robe
Of you, and you held me idly
And above me the slits of your eyes
Fascinated me, they were caves
Of an endless darkness
Your mind wandered, I let it go
Encouraged it, then you came back
Broke into a smile
Came out of the white land
Of speechlessness

VI

I'll be like the sea behind you
happiness thrown away like a coin
the face becoming like anyone else's
your belly on a temple fading away

VII

Now what shall we do with these moments
They are left over from our nights
And they lie upon our skins too heavily.
Feel them though! They are small round circles
Of light that disappear
The pond itself disappears now
The light has lifted off a pair of brown eyes
The night has gone and left excruciating stars
Those moments are gone like coins in the hand
Those moments are simply my mouth
Disappearing off your breast

St. Valentine's Day as Another Chance for Mothers and Fathers to Quarrel

And these stories about my father
that have come down
toppling off the cliff of my aunt's bitterness,
the one about Woolworth's, how there
he bought a giant red heart of chocolates,
how he laid it upon the seat
of the gloom-black Chevrolet, and how
my mother, when he picked her up
from her virtuous employment
saw that box with its satin shine
and my father said "Don't touch that,
those chocolates are for my girl
friend" or how he said something vaguely
and truly like that
and how it was raining sticks and stones;
how when we were starving in the genuine
Thirties he nevertheless treated himself
to T-bone steaks in secret diners,
with frenchfries, how even there he flirted
with the waitresses, pinched one. And how
in a greasy sort of diner, he sat one day,
another girlfriend there across the booth,
when Mother passed by
and caught them, like a window
display of lovers — whereupon he ran
out the backdoor of Tulsa.
Now it is easy
to see they are the stories of a small
woman. He no more loved so well
than she died of cancer like she promised.

Now that the years give me back
the love of my father, I see what is really
important from those years, the black
Chevrolet, a thing in itself, stilled now
so that some chicken may roost
in its seats. And the diner,
where it is, provides an altar
for my memory, and
Woolworth's is a place to love.

Note

Dad,
have no feeling for you anymore
can lay your snapshot on the table
and not be moved to tears
your ancient mustache
and the plaid of your sport-coat collar
your slick tie with the wings of herons
I am unmoved

The Blue Duck

An idea can be glazed, captured, brought down
From heaven!
Our feathers can become blue,
Even a beak can smile!
This duck crouches in a world that cannot
Break it, says Open our eyes,
Let them become luminous,
Amused, and kind!
Duck says to so much: I am not interested.
Duck says Let us feel this blue floating
Down from heaven, let us have thoughts
Between us, let us be fearless.
Duck says Consider the dumbness of animals,
How wonderful it is not to care about death,
To go on falling away from this worst nature
That has been patted upon us like clay.
Duck says We can sit still and go on swimming
Toward the infinite.
Duck says We do not have to judge
With pleasure or displeasure or tell
Ourselves it is all for the best or not.
Duck shows us how naked he is,
How obscene it is to wear a helmet.
Duck says, even to Sunday crowds,
We are lovers, we are without purpose!

Confessions of a Happy Man

I have come to tell you
I am the music of my own defeat,
It is almost breaking
                              me.

How do you stay
And not seem to be destroyed
By these voices, these waters
                    washing round you?

I am the sound of my own defeat,
Neither the flower nor the song blossoming.
I am neither the curtain nor anything
In the room.
I am not a made thing, not a shelter,
Not a note of music,
                    Surely I am not the tapestry
Nor anything fine.

You sit, so absorbed, so oblivious,
As if apprehension had left you long ago,
Made you sit like a silent sea that will never more
Endure a storm. You have created
Some new and original simple-mindedness;
Some ecstasy before which my longing must
Bow down. Even your curls are an invitation
To matters far and long. Your dreams? Yes
Now I see this,

You are set upon by dreams, pinned in
Their golden light, like Saint Sebastian
And his arrows. You sit like a fantastic
Roman saint caught in a wood that survives.
You sit dazed by dreams
                    you've stolen from night.

Whether you have wisdom or merely appear to
Is something I worry about as I travel on.
So I remember your eyes and try to think
On their quality of round seeing.

These are the concerns of years now, of years.
And yet of wisdom you will tell me nothing.
Is it a path worth pursuing?
Is it the deception of a simple child?

When you smile I think we are wholly occupied
With the affable. I dream of going back
To worlds we've left, before I oppressed
The ocean, scarred the sky,
And made myself a pain to women. I look
Over your shoulders
And watch the stars burning, finding in
Them more friendliness, more loneliness.

After Ghalib's Ghazal XXIII, translated with Aijaz Ahmad

Judy, a Face

The face is a
constant; the distances
are forgotten and then
attack again, make
themselves known;
it is quite
literal
the elevation, the
inches
I am above
a face, and the waves
that lie between me
and a face.
My mind
knows the outlay
of miles
and minutes, and how far
the light has fallen
into darkness.
This is the face
always framed
in the hair
or by light only
or by air itself
or by the future's
unfortunate
wooden frame; it is a
face, the face
across the sea;
it is all the structure
hands have been
searching for,
what archeologists
have been trying

to cradle in the hands,
for they have searched
for nothing else
not even in the lakes
of Africa;
and this is what it is
— a face —
what music tries
to find, what the makers
of plots
must weave around;
this face is
the only thing time
has worked
to bring
into the light
and into my hand, a face

Gathering Firewood

This too is a way
of making love, saying
nothing, breaking the sticks
over our knees,
seeing that the green moss
of graveyards is the greenery
of our fire, mingled
eyes. The geese are white
as your blouse. These sticks
cannot be used to beat
us black and blue and tear
our image down all night.
We are breaking them over
our knees, once in a while
smiling

Selected Poems from *X-Rays* and *Dragging the Main*

X-Ray

Strangely
    my mother's sad eyes
        did not show up
           on the X-ray
though I had long since
    swallowed
        all her sorrows
and they should have been
      right there
          where the pain IS

nor my father's
      old loves
      which should have been
      THERE
    cavorting
heedless of fluoroscopic
        voyeurs

nor was the little boy
    loveless and snotnosed
who'd been entombed
    for sure
        there
    years ago
in sight,

Perhaps he hid
    behind the spleen
        behind the ribs
Oh he is out of hiding now
    and is drumming drumming
        drumming my heart.

On Reading That Napoleon Was Poisoned

Science has pinned
Napoleon down
At last,

Those final days
On St. Helena,
The walks, the sea,

And those who worried,
Scanned Europe,
Thought they'd better

Take steps, science
Now confirms, neutron
Analysis shows

From the clipped
Hair of the little
Fellow

That he was poisoned,
Slowly,
Over a period of time,

In his soup,
They thought it
Clever, covered up,

Wiped off the slates
Of history, but
Hair takes into itself

All stories, a man's
Aspirin, his
Arsenic,

And you can be
Tested in a hundred
Years

And they will know
Whether,
When you turned

To me,
Love shot
Through your long hair

The Fourth of July

My uncle,
Great Norman,
Whose leg was full of
Finest German steel,
Broke three chairs and a table
When the kids
Set off firecrackers
On July 4, 1946,
Just after apple pie.

The Card-Players

How we envy their not caring,
        their sculptural crossing of legs,
their idle tossing of cards!
When they get up they are satisfied
as if from work. They rub
                their hands,
        adjust belts,
jingle change in their pockets, and
see that their wives have been loyal
           in their absence.
And all along they have been fishy enough
for a painting by Cezanne.

Midnight

The linoleum has archipelagos of socks
You would have picked up.
My need for your love
Is like an intense, high-pitched
Coded scream that floats out over valleys.
No one sleeping in the farms between us
Can hear this cry for help.
I wonder if you do.
Do you think it is the scream of an animal?

Redburn's Vertigo Compared

He once took delight in the main skysail
But knew it could be more breathless, heavenly—
For moonsails and skyscrapers and cloudrakers
Touch the high winds too. There is no end
To proliferation of fable—canvas and star
A man climbs as he can. And walking
Without you—it never seemed possible—
I know there is no end to woe—by the barn
An old cow is chewing. She can go on chewing
Forever as I can grieve forever
And always a greater grief and a new land.
The heavens are still dizzy with promises.

Coming into Portland

Now we give up the frogpond and the road
And the spring you leant over naked.
We give up the badlands and all
The waitresses bringing us coffee. We stop
One last time by the side of the road—
Stones and moose horns
Before we descend into the plains
And the world once more of the row-houses.
Twice I have thought of the girl in white cowboy boots
Who glanced at me
In Dickinson, North Dakota.

An Egyptian Couple in the Louvre

Their decision brought them beyond their
Points of contact—her hair on his shoulder
The touching arm and hip, the lost embrace.
They have become an eternal mood no war can touch.
That they loved each other no one ever doubted.
That they walk on together through the centuries
Is an established fact, his right hand
Holding her little fist as he steps out toward
The town they knew. This fierce expression on
Their faces has been arrested in light, on their journey.

The Paseo in Irun

It is like Dragging the Main
    in our hotrods   back home
only it is walking
    under umbrellas   taking the Sunday paseo
about 7 P.M.   in early darkness
    the mother or the aunt showing off
the young beauty   in the light of ice
    cream parlors   the lovers thrilling
to the touch   this only time   each week
It is Sunday   and raining
    this is the paseo   in Irun or Pamplona
they stroll   in pairs   the novia
                     and the novio
press each other's   wrists
    and take this sight   permitted
of each other's   night   faces
and moving   lips
And girls go   arm in arm
    throwing dark glances
under the expensive umbrellas   and at the corner
    they swing each other around
with joined arms   as at a Square Dance
               to stroll along
once more   nothing
gets accomplished   except
    what is seen   on a face

the girl sitting on the bench and the
man standing above her with his hands
hopelessly in his pockets are having
a hard time of it. His eyes are almost
as red as hers are and he goes on saying
things with a kind of run-down version
of his usual charm. But she's fed up,
and looking between overcoats, toying
with the green umbrella in a smoke-
filled station, is one more way of
keeping from crying. She gets up
to leave with a vengeance. His hand
touches her, and he makes her smile
once more, using torture. She'd still
die for him. She reads his face again
like a book she's put down a thousand
thousand times. Now she obeys
and steps up onto that wooden train
past numbers painted gold. This
is a train heading through mountains.
When she settles herself by the window
she is already broadcasting to other
men the message of her helplessness.

The Art Museum

I hated to leave
        Epstein's woman
            on the stair
And evidence in the Fragonard
        that my son too would
            have his day
And be gone

Along with the woman I almost
        broke away from my friends
    .   to speak to boldly

Outside, the faces of waitresses
        are immortal and in bronze
I get confused and cannot accept
        the passing faces
            for what they are

At the Washing of My Son

I ran up and grabbed your arm, the way a man
On a battlefield would recognize a long-lost comrade.
You were still wrinkled, and had a hidden face,
Like a hedgehog or a mouse, and you crouched in
The black elbows of a Negro nurse. You were
Covered with your mother's blood, and I saw
That navel where you and I were joined to her.
I stood by the glass and watched you squeal.
Just twice in a man's life there's this
Scrubbing off of blood. And this holy
Rite that Mother Superior in her white starched hat
Was going to deny me. But I stood my ground.
And then went in where for the first time you felt
Your mother's face, and her open blouse.

The Waves

FOR WESLEY

Where the waves show their teeth
    the way Hokusai made them
       or saw them
You point, just two years old now,
    and say "Here comes another one!"
You speak with particular reverence
      for just that wave,
Giving me a moment I can take to the next world.

On Seeing a Movie Based on an Episode from President Kennedy's Life

Tonight we took
the boys to see
PT Boat 1
09 at the
Dryden Drive-In
3 boys in the
Volkswagen and
our daughter of
course. Before that
we had to watch
Bob Mitchum chase
a tiger with
a torch and then
like Wilson in
Hemingstein's best
story steal the
girl indifferent
ly. Jack Hawkins
tried to shoot him
too. The boys sd
this was scary.
In the next car
a man shoved his
girl down in the
seat and had at
her; I turned the
mirror and watched
his shirt going

up and down, it
took about eight
or ten minutes.
Maybe it was
their first time, they
lit cigarettes
then Jack, dead Jack
came on and we
saw him choose his
PT boat, paint
er up and head
for battle. Av
rom had to pee
just then and wd
nt go outside
on the gravel
so we had to
leave. I loved Jack
Kennedy, he
wanted better
for us than these
Drive-In thumpings.
Under the great
stars of Amer
ica there shd
be better. We
were choked on car
fumes; to go down
town wd be worse.
On the way home
we passed trailer
parks, the sad young

marrieds inside
watching TV.
Why shdn't they
give up and hug
in those shoebox
havens, pullman
bunks and porta
ble blue heavens
if they can't walk
out into the
night without get
ting gassed? They know
their dreams are put
to sleep like pups.

Moment by the Sea

You ask me if it's lava
That's stopped here,
At the sea, if it's fire
That's bubbled and cooled,
Because of the sea,
Into these great chunks.
I don't know, and answer
"I suppose so." We join
Hands and walk in
The shadows of the rock's
History, kick a few
Pebbles on the sand.
Thinking of someone else
I decide it was not so casual,
The way she betrayed me,
That it was a grief
Burning out only now in
Your strange and cooling presence.

Some Notes on Viet-Nam

I.

Carpaccio saw all this —
        a gang of armed ruffians
falling to it: the arrow in the throat
        the sword in the belly
the knife through the cheek, the left
        hand pulling the woman's hair
to bring her throat to the broadsword.

Even the trees seem to writhe away
from the slaughter of the innocents.
But nobody notices the trees.

II.

What have they brought to the streets
        of Saigon except smog
and for the kids lessons on how to suck?
The booted Green Beret thinks he is
        after all the uphill hero
        of Salerno.
These *are* the end-of-the-world days
        and that black kite or crow
in a tree in Spain is no bird or iron-
        sculpture, but a dark sign of the end
the spilled radioactive junk, the unconcern.

III.

It is time to honor the old Fascists.
So *Life* looks up Mama Mussolini
and adores her steaming spaghetti.
And the *West Point Atlas of American Wars*
uses the *Nazi* general, von Paulus, at Stalingrad
for *its* Horatio at the Bridge example.

IV.

The inductees cross the country in one night
so the men and women sleeping in small towns below them
will not know what a tidal movement
of armed men is flooding the world.
They pay half fare like college students
and sit dazed over coffee at 3 A.M. waiting
for the next plane. They talk of Saigon
in the men's room, like some girl
they've had — those who have been with her
and those on the way.
They take with them their inability to love.
They do not sense the dark generations
saying things under the rice.

V.

Under the snow old warriors of 1940
are smiling. So they took Stalingrad after all
and cut down all the birches
and made the minds of the people dream of cars.
Now the rivers are beginning to gleam
like rainbows and smell of American oil.

Doing Without

's an interesting
custom, involving such in-
visible items as the food
that's not on the table, the clothes
that are not on the back
the radio whose only music
is silence. Doing without
is a great protector of reputations
since all places one cannot go
are fabulous, and only the rare and
enlightened plowman in his field
or on his mountain does not overrate
what he does not or cannot have.
Saluting through their windows
of cathedral glass those restaurants
we must not enter (unless like
burglars we become subject to
arrest) we greet with our twinkling
eyes the faces of others who do
without, the lady with the
fishing pole, and the man who looks
amused to have discovered on a walk
another piece of firewood.

Committee

Men have through all ages sat in council
And sometimes around tables, Homeric
Men, and standing men, Indians, and these
Men in their dark ties. We are in a circle
And talking in a circle and making the
Choices of our lives:

> backache,
> the green blackboard,
> the pipe to be chewed,
> the cough drop, the bitter lemon,
> the coil of red cellophane
> around the finger,
> Paper Topics,
> sad doodles of cages and zigzags,
> the Regional Report,
> sinus-carrying Nile sludge,
> no place to spit,
> all the windows closed,
> backache,
> courtyard brick,
> a report from the other committee,
> the sun moving away as if appalled,

All afternoon on the ship where there is no leader
and the garrulous lap at us like endless ocean
waves, insignificant and tireless.
Sometimes around this magnificent table
Men who have always been dull and defeated
Seem to take on life as they say "It seems to me ..."
Or "I should think ..." or "If you ask me ..." (Nobody did)
Often we get up as if we'd decided where
To send our frogmen or how to scale the wall.
But no one can find a wall or name a sea.

Dragging the Main

In the town by the sea I walked
Past the closed beauty shops where the
Hair-driers inside gleamed like bombs
And the mannikins wearing their human
Hair didn't understand this game:
The cars drove round and round the
City blocks, their hoods and trunks
Leaded in and young eyes burned
Like radar above the red fires of cigarettes.

I looked through bakery shops and
Laundromats, searched the stark lights
The put-down baskets, the dizzy doors
For answers. I walked on as they revved
Away. We moved at our different speeds
Through rows of hot-dog stands,
Amusement arcades, pinball games, and doubled
Back. I saw the girl alone
In her car, and she turned to glance
At me. I thought the love that had
Once thrown me away was sneaking up
On four tires and about to say Honey

You get right in here. I waved.
She sped up and her taillight bobbed
Three blocks away through the mist.
I stopped under the marquee, turned
Again at the Watch Repair
Then saw her eyes again. They were not
Like those floating eyes of fish

That stared from the other cars.
She *knew* me, but something kept her
From slowing, and made her gawk and appraise.
She was brunette, and all by herself
And passed me five, ten, twenty times.
I waved from the bridge.

Each time I thought I'd lost her
Her gaze honked upon me once more.
Twice in the dark I raced her till
I stood where the Shell sign squeaked.
I breathed deep that perfume she left
And was glad she helped to destroy me.

More and more she floated past in shadows.
I was chained to her recurring course.
I was *faithful*. She spoke to me
Lowering for once the window of cold
Glass and we were there by the roaring sea.
She said it wasn't love stinging my face
But only the pure cars of America that
Were dragging the main, looking for fools
Who want to hold even the lights of Main
Street, and the sweetness of a face.

The Family in the Hills

I don't believe in modern times, I believe in those times.
Still the heartbreak, still no view of the sea.
Still the child in the arms, the bare feet, the bewildered
Look away from the sun.
I have not gone forward into the years of light.
I have fallen back into those years.
For the touch of those arms I would have to go backward
Face by face, arm by arm, through a thousand failures.
Why not start at the beginning? With the first sadness.